YOUR KNOWLEDGE HAS VALUE

- We will publish your bachelor's and master's thesis, essays and papers

- Your own eBook and book - sold worldwide in all relevant shops

- Earn money with each sale

Upload your text at www.GRIN.com and publish for free

Bibliographic information published by the German National Library:

The German National Library lists this publication in the National Bibliography; detailed bibliographic data are available on the Internet at http://dnb.dnb.de .

This book is copyright material and must not be copied, reproduced, transferred, distributed, leased, licensed or publicly performed or used in any way except as specifically permitted in writing by the publishers, as allowed under the terms and conditions under which it was purchased or as strictly permitted by applicable copyright law. Any unauthorized distribution or use of this text may be a direct infringement of the author s and publisher s rights and those responsible may be liable in law accordingly.

Imprint:

Copyright © 2014 GRIN Verlag, Open Publishing GmbH
Print and binding: Books on Demand GmbH, Norderstedt Germany
ISBN: 9783668371286

This book at GRIN:

http://www.grin.com/en/e-book/350576/are-human-rights-merely-western-constructions

Anna Scheithauer

Are Human Rights "Merely" Western Constructions?

A Case Against Cultural Relativism

GRIN Publishing

GRIN - Your knowledge has value

Since its foundation in 1998, GRIN has specialized in publishing academic texts by students, college teachers and other academics as e-book and printed book. The website www.grin.com is an ideal platform for presenting term papers, final papers, scientific essays, dissertations and specialist books.

Visit us on the internet:

http://www.grin.com/

http://www.facebook.com/grincom

http://www.twitter.com/grin_com

Are Human Rights „merely" Western Constructions?

I will take "Western" as a notion corresponding to both the geographical and historical origins of human rights. I will not, though, associate it with the values deriving from the content of human rights. Such, I will refer to as "universal". This is because they go beyond any particular regional considerations. I shall explain this below.

Philosophical contemplations and geopolitical issues relating to arguments of imperialism and external imposition of human rights, won't concern us here. They will, therefore, be excluded from discussion. This is due to the genetic fallacy these considerations are prone to, when used as arguments for "Western" parochialism; a term used for referring to "Western" standards as "local prescription, posing as a universal value system". (Meckled-Garcia in Scheithauer, 2013, 22) Just because the concept of human rights has its particular origins, it does not follow that its underlying ideas and values are tainted. (Halliday, 1995, 166)

In this essay, I shall focus on the very content of human rights, thereby, relating to the debate between universalist and cultural relativist theory. While the former promotes the idea of equal rights for all human beings and considers culture irrelevant for the validity of moral rights, the latter views culture as the exclusive source of moral rights (Donelly, 1984, 400) and stresses, that "right" and "wrong" differ from culture to culture. (Tilley, 2000, 501)

In the light of this debate, I will argue, that human rights are not merely "Western" constructions, as they withstand, despite their historical and geographical significance, accusations of cultural superiority (Tilley, 2000, 527) and of evaluations of other cultures according to the terms and conditions of "Western" culture (Oxford Dictionaries, 2013), or in short: of "Western" ethnocentrism.

I will hold this premise as response specifically to the allegation of cultural insensitivity brought forward by cultural relativism, which emphasizes human rights' ignorance towards cultural complexities by prioritizing some values over others, thereby, disregarding the collective spirit of some communities. This is said to render the concept of human rights inapplicable in non-"Western" societies. In this sense, property rights, family rights and religious rights, focusing on the individual rather than the tribe, clan or any other collectivity, are said to be particularly incompatible. (Cerna, 1994, 746) Moreover, proponents of this argument point to human rights as destroying local culture in that they exhibit a lack of tolerance for local customs and traditions. Campaigning, in the name of human rights, against morally grotesque practices with deep cultural roots such as Female Genital Mutilation (FGM) can be taken as one example of many for such intolerance. (Scheithauer, 2013, 22)

I will counter-argue that the human rights conception is culturally *sensitive,* as it recognizes diversity of moral views by promoting freedom of choice and the inclusion of voices otherwise left unheard under the umbrella of collectivism. Thereby, I will show that universal values can indeed be justified, while cultural relativism fails to provide a sufficient explanation for moral validity. In this respect, I shall challenge the term "culture" and will show that human rights advocate tolerance. They do so through their stress on the preservation of cultural pluralism. Thus, they are not set out to destroy local culture but rather arguments of authority; of political elites, who propagate extreme conservatism in order to further their self-interest while ignoring the needs for moral progress in their country. (Tesón, 1985, 388) Hence, proponents of human rights demonstrate a desire not to seem narrow minded and to offer protections for the particularly vulnerable in society. (Scheithauer, 2013, 21)

From this I will conclude, that the premise set out above holds true. Consequently, human rights by upholding universal moral values and by promoting cultural diversity, despite their geographical and historical distinctiveness, are more than "Western" constructions.

Cultural Insensitivity: To Whom?

Human rights are often said to be culturally insensitive, representing a "Western" concept and reflecting "Western" values, which are considered incompatible with the values of non-"Western" societies, and therefore, cannot be justified to them. (Erez, 2013) This cultural relativist claim is based on the assumption that morals vary with cultural norms and stresses the importance to maintain cultural diversity. (Tilley, 2000, 501) This brings up the question of why the belonging to a specific cultural community is morally relevant. We certainly don't choose which environment we are born into. Consequently, there's no reason why we deserve or should be held responsible for our place of birth or cultural community rendering our cultural context irrelevant to our moral worth. (Tesón, 1985, 386) In this spirit, universalism - by its critics referred to as "Western" outlook - promulgates the universal validity of some moral judgements, and with it the idea of human rights as equal rights for all human beings. (Tilley, 2000, 505)

The core issue of this debate relates to the question of compatibility of values, as cultural relativists argue, human rights with their emphasis on individual rights ignore cultural complexities as, i.e. they aren't obviously applicable in communities following a collectivist approach. Not only do they focus on the individual, but completely neglect communal rights. For example, everyone's right to own property clashes with social ownership, a concept, where land is owned collectively. (Pollis and Schwab, 1979, 17) But, with view to such incompatibility, the dilemma only starts when cases of discrimination, marginalization and exclusion arise under such collective spirit. For instance, in many cultures women are prohibited from owing property including its inheritance. The cultural relativist sees nothing wrong in this, justifying the practice in terms of his/her cultural norms. But by systematically excluding some of its participants in the name of culture, the relativist refutes himself, as it is him, who has become the culturally insensitive one, hindering culture from flourishing to its full extent. (Scheithauer, 2013, 21)

In this sense, the biggest challenges, however, rest in the private sphere, especially regarding family and religious rights. The former provides for full age and "free and full consent" of both partners upon marriage. Further, it guarantees for religious, national and racial non-discrimination, equal rights in marriage and upon its dissolution, as well as to found a family. (Universal Declaration, 1948) Relativists claim that these provisions demonstrate a clear disregard for different moral views and with it for certain cultural practices and traditions, since these rights are neither compatible with practices of arranged and underage marriage, nor with some Islamic conceptions prohibiting interfaith marriage, nor with certain family planning strategies such as i.e. female infanticide. Here, the matter is of similar nature, centering on exclusion from decision-making. But by precluding certain voices from speaking out, the danger arises that people's conformity with cultural norms is a result of coercion rather than conviction. (Meckled-Garcia, 2013)

This exemplifies, that cultural relativism by determining the rightness of an act by one's cultural norms (Tilley, 2000, 527), doesn't allow for differing moral views, whereas universalist provisions, promoting free choice, respect the moral views of others. In the case above, by requiring the coming of age to enable self-determination, the necessity for "free and full consent" (Universal Declaration, 1948) aiming at the authenticity of decisions made, anti-discrimination regulations to open up the pool of choices, and equal rights provisions to guarantee fair conditions for decision-making.

Similar observations can be made with view to the right to freedom of religion, whose provision to freely change one's religion/belief, has earned heavy critique, especially from the Islamic countries, which consider it incompatible with their faith and punishable by death. However, it is to note that the ones invoking the Quran and sharia in this way, don't represent the whole Islamic world: i.e. Turkey has engaged in secularizing its laws. This demonstrates progress in the compatibility of human rights with cultural complexities. Also, there is no one Islamic body of thought, nor is there one central authority representing the whole Muslim religion (Halliday, 1995, 155-156). This indicates a certain possibility for flexibility in interpretation, and in turn, for congruency of Islamic values with universal human rights provisions. In fact, the moderate version of the Islamic faith is found compatible with values of equality and religious freedom, stressing to take into account present-day conditions. (Scheithauer, 2009, 6)

This shows, that cultures are not only diverse, but also dynamic. We have come to see that there is no such thing as a Muslim position; equally there is no "African" or "Asian" stance as such, as each region in itself is imprinted by different legal, political and religious systems. (Halliday, 1995, 155-156) Also, we can infer from the above that cultural traditionalism refutes itself in that cultures evolve over time, so that each traditionalist inevitably deviates from something preceding. (Scheithauer, 2009, 5) This indicates that moral progress is not only possible but happening. In this respect, cultural relativism falls short of an explanation, for moral truth is said to rest in one's cultural norms, which outlaws the challenging of practices - and with it moral progress - that are entrenched in our culture. (Tilley, 2000, 512)

The paragraphs above suggest, that the challenge lies not so much with the justification of universal values in different societies but rather with their implementation in culturally sensitive ways. (Scheithauer, 2013, 22) Because, - as we have come to see - human rights don't aim to reduce everyone to a single pattern of life, but strive to promote diversity. (Jones, 1994, 214) In fact, most people around the globe accept the validity of some universal moral values such as i.e. freedom from torture, slavery and starvation. This is because acts of torture, slavery or starvation cannot be attributed to any particular local culture as opposed to other practices, which have deep cultural roots. (Donnelly, 1984, 413) But then, the question is, where do we draw the line? And, does a line have to be drawn at all? (Halliday, 1995, 163)

In order to answer these questions, let's consider the practice of FGM. Not only is it immensely painful, but leaves young girls traumatized and inalterably disfigured. (Tamir, 2006) As the practice is prescribed by cultural norms, cultural relativists view it as morally justified, whereas universalist proponents of human rights vehemently object to it, regarding the practice a threat to foremost an individual's life and bodily integrity. Here, I suggest to shift the debate to the level of values, which underly the motivation for the practice to see, if reconciliation of both views is possible. While some universal values have been laid out, the cultural relativist stance has so far only engaged in circular reasoning by equating its conclusion with the premise, in the sense that "what my culture says is morally right" and "it is morally right what my culture says". By doing so, it fails to provide a test for moral validity and with it a justification for also the practice of FGM. (Scheithauer, 2013, 23) When we come to speak of values prompting FGM, the most named by cultural relativists are hygiene, virginity upon marriage and marital fidelity. (Midwives, 2009/10) But these are, indeed, universal values going beyond cultural particularities, featuring a broad leeway for their realization. Therefore, the practice of FGM cannot be considered a necessary consequential result.

This illustrates, that cultural relativists and universalists are certain to meet on the level of values. Accordingly no line needs to be drawn. Nevertheless, this is not the end of the debate, as cultural relativists will argue, that human rights destroy local culture and, consequently, a community's stability through their intolerance of communal customs and traditions. (Scheithauer, 2013, 22) However, culture itself cannot said to be destroyed, because, as explained, it is nothing static. This is not to deny, of course, that human rights might disrupt the traditional system. (Donnelly, 1984, 419) But when coming to speak of traditional customs and practices, we need to ask if human rights put a stop to something valuable or important, and if stability is upheld in a genuine way.

Especially, when considering that cultural relativism cannot provide a rational for why we should do what our culture says, there is sufficient reason to feel alert. Cultural relativism often serves as a typical argument of authority to prevent positive change for the masses. (Tesón, 1985, 388) While government officials propagate against "Western" individualism, they have long left traditionalism behind, filling their pockets with massive profits from corruption, send their loved ones to study in American and European Universities, and consume "Western" luxury goods. At the same time, they carry out development policies, which undermine traditional communities. For example, by producing cash crops instead of food, widespread malnutrition is caused by political elites under the umbrella of collectivism. We can agree, that this doesn't exemplify a genuine expression of indigenous culture. Proponents of cultural relativism support this universalist stance, when proclaiming that human rights violations by the regime are not only antithetical to "Western" human rights conceptions, but also to a community's cultural traditions. (Donelly, 1984, 411-413)

In this sense, cultural relativists are correct when attributing an element of destruction to the concept of human rights. Nevertheless, they fail to acknowledge that human rights don't aim to destroy local culture as such, but arguments of authority, evoking practices that cannot be justified. Toleration only ends when a practice is deemed so morally grotesque, that it isn't worth keeping! Thereby, it is important to distinguish intolerance from interference, since the former doesn't automatically induce the latter. Interference depends on many other things than a practice's moral status, such as how harmful a practice is and if the outcome would be favorable. (Tilley, 2000, 543) In this respect, human rights strive to maintain cultural pluralism and offer protections for the vulnerable in society, particularly when a regime fails to do so. They put emphasis on the necessity to keep an open mind for divergent moral views and stress the importance to implement these provisions in culturally sensitive ways.

Conclusion

We have come to see that human rights, despite their geographical and historical distinctiveness, are not merely "Western" constructions in that they uphold universal moral values, applicable across cultures and valid on an equal basis for all human beings. Thus, the evaluation of other cultures goes beyond the terms and conditions of "Western" culture, which rules out all criticism of cultural superiority. In this respect, I have shown, that human rights promote cultural diversity and are culturally sensitive in that they recognize different moral views through the advocacy of freedom of choice and inclusion, by accentuating the notion of tolerance with their stress on the necessity for the preservation of cultural pluralism, and by enabling for moral progress and protection for the vulnerable, when challenging arguments of authority. It is for these reasons, that the cultural relativist accusation of "Western" ethnocentrism, and with it the allegation of cultural insensitivity, is unsustainable.

Bibliography

Cerna, C. (1994) "Universality of Human Rights and Cultural Diversity: Implementation of Human Rights in Different Socio-Cultural Contexts", Human Rights Quarterly, Vol. 16, No. 4, Baltimore: The John Hopkins University Press, pp. 740-752

Donnelly, J. (1984) "Cultural Relativism and Universal Human Rights", Human Rights Quarterly, Vol. 6, No. 4, Baltimore: The Johns Hopkins University Press, pp. 400-419

Erez, L. (2013) "The Case for Cultural Relativism", Handout, Theoretical Foundations of Human Rights, Fall Semester, University College London

Halliday, F. (1995) "Relativism and Universalism in Human Rights: The Case of the Islamic Middle East", Beetham, D., eds., (1995) *Politics and Human Rights,* Oxford: Blackwell, pp. 152-167

Jones, P. (1994) "Some Doubts and Difficulties", Rights, pp. 213-220

Scheithauer, A. (2013) "Classnotes", *Lecture/Seminar Notes,* Theoretical Foundations of Human Rights, Fall Semester , University College London

Scheithauer, A. (2009) " Internationale Menschenrechte: Entzieht sich die UDHR durch Einberaumung der Artikel 18 und 27 selbst ihren Anspruch auf den universalen Gültigkeitsbereich der Menschenrechte? - Eine Aufarbeitung anhand des Beispiels Islam", Research Paper for Seminar BA 2.3: Methoden und Elemente des politikwissenschaftlichen Denkens und Arbeitens, Fall Semester, University of Vienna

Pollis, A. and Schwab, P. (1979) "Human Rights: A Western Construct with Limited Applicability", Human Rights: Cultural and Ideological Perspectives, New York: Praeger, pp. 1-18

Tamir, Y. (2006) "Hands off Clitoridectomy", Boston Review, June 1, viewed 18 December 2013, http://www.bostonreview.net/yael-tamir-hands-off-clitoridectomy

Tesón, F. (1985) "International Human Rights and Cultural Relativism", Virginia Journal of International Law, Vol. 25. Virginia: University of Virginia Press, pp. 379-396

Tilley, J. (2000) "Cultural Relativism", Human Rights Quarterly, Vol. 22, No. 2, May, Baltimore: The Johns Hopkins University Press, pp. 501-547

Oxford Dictionaries (2013) "Ethnocentric", Oxford: Oxford University Press, viewed 18 December 2013, http://www.oxforddictionaries.com/definition/english/ethnocentric

Meckled-Garcia, S. (2013), E-mail correspondence: s.meckled-garcia@ucl.ac.uk, "PUBLG075: Today's Lecture - The Punchline", December 6

Midwives. (2009/10) "Female Genital Mutilation", Midwives magazine, viewed 18 December 2013, http://www.rcm.org.uk/midwives/in-depth-papers/female-genital-mutilation/

UN General Assembly. (1948) Universal Declaration of Human Rights, 10 December, 217 A (III), http://www.un.org/en/documents/udhr/

YOUR KNOWLEDGE HAS VALUE

- We will publish your bachelor's and master's thesis, essays and papers

- Your own eBook and book - sold worldwide in all relevant shops

- Earn money with each sale

Upload your text at www.GRIN.com
and publish for free